Peter Saves For A Rainy Day

DEDICATED TO MY FAVORITE BOY —
MY CREATIVE AND IMAGINATIVE SON, VITO
WITH LOTS OF LOVE FROM MAMA

One fine day a little boy named Peter was born.

Mama and Papa brought little Peter home.
At first, all that Peter did was eat and sleep.

His parents were so excited to have a new baby
they decided to throw a welcome party for him.
They invited all their family and friends.

Peter received many gifts — a teddy bear ...
a piggy bank ... a red truck ... and lots of other
toys and stuffed animals.

Some relatives brought envelopes with money and checks, which are pieces of paper just like money. His parents put all the money into the bank to save it for little Peter's future.

Peter was growing up. He met other little boys and
girls in his neighborhood. He loved playing with the
other children.

14

When Peter was able to walk, his parents took him to a big grey building. They said they were taking him to a bank, but he didn't know what that meant.

As they entered the building, Peter looked up at everything. He saw lots of people working behind windows at countertops. Peter's parents lined up to talk to one of the people who worked at the window openings.

When it was his family's turn, he grabbed for the colorful lollipops on the counter. His parents let him take a raspberry lollipop, which was delicious.

When little Peter got older, his grandparents bought him a toy cash register. It was filled with all sorts of play money. There were green paper dollar bills with the numbers for ten, five, and one on them. There were also toy silver dimes, nickels, and quarters. Peter loved playing with the pretend money and using it to buy toy food.

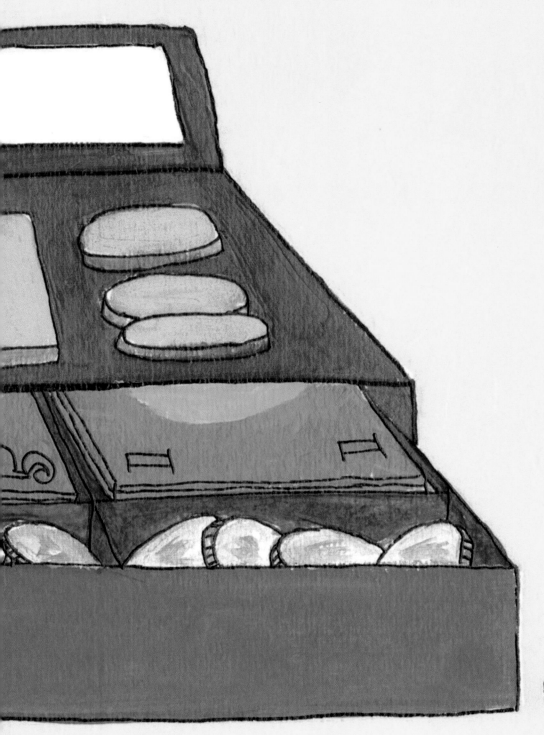

Soon little Peter started school. He learned his ABCs and his 123s. He loved his teachers and he liked learning the alphabet and all about numbers.

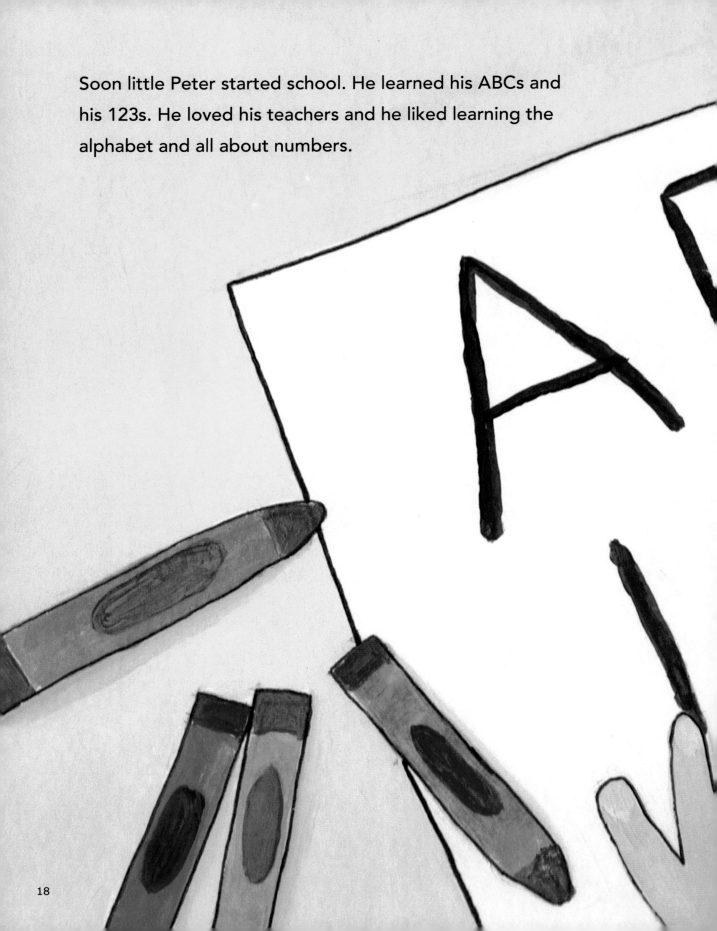

One day, little Peter and his parents were driving by the big grey building where he always got his lollipops.
"Why do you go to this big building?" he asked them.
"That building is a bank," his mother answered.
"When we work at our jobs, we earn money and it goes into the bank to be saved for us. The bank keeps it safe."

"That's right," Papa added. "It's important to save our money for a rainy day." Peter was confused. "Why do we need money when it rains?" he asked. Mama and Papa chuckled. "Saving money for a rainy day is an expression," Papa explained. "It means that when something new happens that we may not have expected — like a

sudden rainstorm or anything we didn't predict — it's nice to have money sitting safely in the bank for us." "When the unexpected happens, like something breaking and needing to be fixed, then families need money to pay for it," Papa continued, "and that's why it's important to have extra money in the bank."

Every day Peter would go to school, practice writing his letters and numbers. He wondered what job he wanted when he grew up.

After dinner the next night the doorbell rang.
Ding! Dong! "Oh, look, it's Mrs. Monroe," said Mama
to Peter, as they opened the door.

Mama introduced Peter to Mrs. Monroe, who took out some papers, books, and a calculator. "Mama, what does Mrs. Monroe do for work?" Peter asked. "Well, remember when Mama told you that when we work, we save our money in the bank?" "Yes, Mama," Peter answered.

"Well, the money goes into the bank so that we can pay for the things we need, like our house, our car, our clothes, and our food.

But the rest goes to Mrs. Monroe and she saves it for us. She is our money advisor — that means that she's our money helper."

"Where does she work?" Peter asked.

"Mrs. Monroe works at an office that's near our bank, and she saves our money for the future."

"Mama, I have an idea," Peter suddenly announced, jumping up with a glint in his eye.

Peter ran to his bedroom and got the cash register that his grandparents had given him.

He brought it back to the living room and showed it to Mama and Mrs. Monroe. Carefully, he opened up its drawer and reached deep inside.

With that, he scooped up all his green paper money and silver coins and threw them up in the air.

He laughed as he called out, "Let's all save our money for a rainy day!"

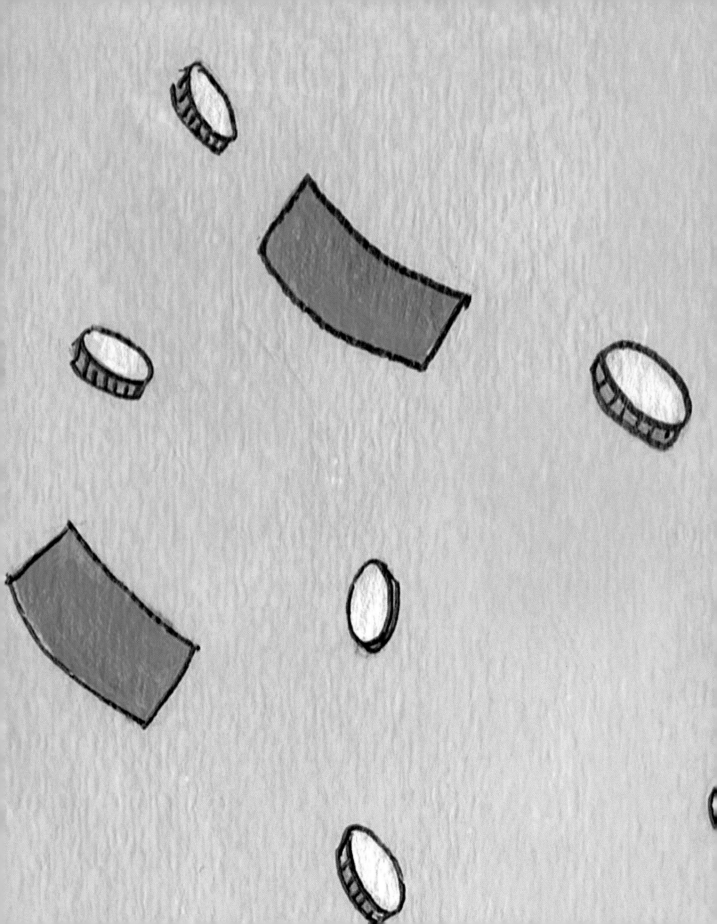

This book was inspired by my seven-year-old son. Through him, I realized how smart, creative, and imaginative children can be, and how teaching them the basics about money can enhance their understanding of the world right from the start.

Not many people find what they love to do at a young age. However, I was blessed to find my dream job at the age of twenty-one. My career journey began while working towards a degree in accounting at Brooklyn College. I was soon offered an internship at a financial company as an assistant to an advisor, and quickly realized that my three favorite things to do were speaking, teaching, and working with people. I found my calling and became a financial advisor. After graduating from college, I began working for a company called *Strategies for Wealth*, where I continue to work today. As a financial advisor, I help clients to achieve their financial goals and I value the close and enduring relationships with all of them.

Along with being a financial advisor, I was lucky enough to become a mother. Over time, I soon realized that my son was listening to the financial advice that I was giving my clients. He would sometimes repeat it back to me, grasping certain financial concepts even at his young age. It became clear that in order for advisors to help future clients reach their fullest financial potential, we needed to start with the children, and create an educational movement. Just like children learn their ABCs and 123s, they can learn the basics of saving for a rainy day and for the future. I began to see how important it is to create financial literacy, especially amongst our young children.

With all of this in mind, my book idea was born. As fate would have it, my illustrator happened to be the daughter of my very first client. This is where it all came together, and I realized what I wanted to do next. I hope you enjoy this book as much as I enjoyed writing it with my son.
— Rosanna Guardavaccaro